Bright Blessings

Suzie Palmer

ISBN 978-81-8253-495-7

First Edition: 2014, Second Edition: 2015

Rs. 150/-

Cyberwit.net

HIG 45 Kaushambi Kunj, Kalindipuram

Allahabad - 211011 (U.P.) India

http://www.cyberwit.net

Tel: +(91) 9415091004 +(91) (532) 2552257

E-mail: info@cyberwit.net

Printed at Repro India Limited.

Dedication

The poems in 'Bright Blessings' are the culmination of my creations between 2009 and 2014. The book starts with my most recent poems and works backwards to 2009. It closes with a collection of haiku, included here in no specific chronological order.

Every poem was written with love and passion, aspiring to reach your heart and unite us all. I send love and joy to all my family and friends near and far… To all people everywhere, you are my family of friends… We are family… inseparable by our inherent oneness of living… By our love we are free. _/I_ Thank you for sharing this precious moment. ♥

FOREWORD

The latest poetry collection 'Bright Blessings' by Suzie Palmer, famous Australian author and poet, reveals the poet's grandeur of imagination. These poems show very apt choice of words and musical cadence. There is no doubt that the style of Suzie in these poems is unquestionably the secret of her power. Her style is full of clarity, simplicity, versatility, passion and spontaneity. This is quite evident in the following lines from the poem "Human Forest":

God is living everywhere
All around us God is there
Lighting hearts like an ember
In the Human Forest of Learning to Care

"Souls-United" is the poem in which her reflection is the boldest:

Fly onwards, forwards, upwards, free
Fly to bridge humanity
Fly with all our hearts and souls
Fly Souls-United
The Journey of Gold

No doubt, the world will be a better place to live in if we "Fly Souls-United". Dylan Thomas aptly remarks: "A good poem is a contribution to reality. The world is never the same once a good poem has been added to it. A good poem helps to change the shape of the universe, helps to extend everyone's knowledge of himself and the world around him." This is quite true about Suzie Palmer's poems that have power "to change the shape of the universe".

Most of the poems included in 'Bright Blessings' are miraculous and full of mellifluousness. It is true that Suzie Palmer in the poem "Fits like a Glove" is quite aware of sanctity of an individual's inner divinity:

Enter into the kingdom
Of God's Love
Divinity within
And, surrounding
Fits like a glove

We feel moments of miraculous experience when we discover the power of "true human might" in the poem "Awaiting a Friend":

One who's seen the light
Of true human might
The spirit that's in you

Robert Frost remarks: "A complete poem is one where an emotion has found its thought and the thought has found the words." This critical observation is truly applicable to Suzie Palmer's poetry.

This collection 'Bright Blessings' also includes haiku, the Japanese poetic form famous throughout the world. The characteristic quality of Suzie Palmer as a haiku poet is her ability to provide impressive and attractive insights. Suzie Palmer is one of the greatest and most famous haiku poets. The diction and apt choice of subtle phrases in these haiku poems is quite admirable. The poet in her simple and unsophisticated haiku is able to write with spontaneity and intuitiveness. Her haiku poems with two subtle images in juxtaposition reveal her poetic maturity:

'Fall!'
Shouted the thunder
To the rain

Written words
Travel world
When legs cannot

- Santosh Kumar

Editor, Cyberwit.net

Contents

Bright Blessings Haiku

Within These Pages

Within these pages are poems from my heart
My own blend of Bright Blessings
Love, I wish to impart

Permeating the world with loving-kindness
Uniting souls through meaningful rhyme
Reminding us of our inherent oneness
May we walk in time, celebrating our chimes

Within these pages are poems from my heart
Bridging life with Bright Blessings
Sending care for all people from the start

¨♫♪ ♥ ♪♫*¨*

Eternal Kings

Past, present, future
Live in the eternal now
All we have is this moment
What is it that makes your heart flower?

Manifest the future
Bring it to your now
Learn from the past, may it soothe you
Never cause you to cower

Brilliance is found in simply being
In this space we're in
Beauty blossoms in our presence
And, being present we are timeless kings

¨♫♪ ♥ ♪♫*¨*

Come Fly with Me

Come fly with me to a land that's free
Exploring vast field's of the fertile mind
Fly with me, consciously
Our imaginations are ready all of the time

Come fly with me: it's liberty
To broaden the expanse of our minds
Fly with me, creatively
We are nothing short of divine

¨♫♪ ♥ ♪♫*¨*

Poetry

A deep expression of the human mind
The instrument of poetry unites all of our kind
Blossoming of friendship, a tool for dialogues
The universal art of poetry, celebrates all of our songs

¨♫♪ ♥ ♪♫*¨*

Happiness

'If you want to be happy Be' ~ Tolstoy

Happiness is a state of mind
When we observe ourselves closely we find
The key is within us all the time
Unlocking our joy uplifts us, sublime

Our happiness affects the entire world
Every sister, boy, brother, and girl
The pursuit of happiness, a primary human goal
Considering the well-being of All enables this goal to excel

Happiness is our intimate gift
Share it with others abundantly to live
In a world promoting fairness and sustainability
Happiness abounds within the world's great family

¨♫♪ ♥ ♪♫*¨*

Your Tale

It's never too late to reignite hope
A ceaselessly, unending determination to cope
Inspiring vision beyond the horizon's line
Moving towards it, the sun eventually shines

Never too late to abandon ship
Reckless and off course, in the end it will sink
By a giant leap of faith, your life you're sure to save
Paving the way to a brighter, better day

Never too late to believe in you
It's really the only worthwhile thing to do
The love inside yourself, is the glowing and precious pearl
Uncovering your own mystery is your tale to tell

¨♫♪ ♥ ♪♫*¨*

Human Halo

'Be kind whenever possible. It is always possible.' ~ Dalai Lama

Kindness is beauty
Kindliness is king
Instigates the beautiful bridge of all forgiving

Kindness is eternal, shining the light
The goodness inside beacons dark nights

Express kindheartedness whenever you can
That magical power of a helping hand

Uplifts the spirit, saves many souls
Kindness illuminates the human halo

¨♫♪ ♥ ♪♫*¨*

Love's Measure

Even a small expression of love
Can equate to so very much
When the meaning is real and true
Love's power shines deeply through

Any darkness or deep crevice
Love finds its way
Love is the reason for life
Brilliantly lights any grey day

Even a small expression of love
Can equate to so very much
Lighten life with your love
Uplifts us up above

¨♫♪ ♥ ♪♫*¨*

Fly

Free human rights
Let the bird out of the cage
May wings of peace
Embrace the entire world's stage

We know the rights of one
Are the rights of all
All people are united
Together we fly or we fall

¨♫♪ ♥ ♪♫*¨*

Glide

A little poem of beauty
A huge message of love
Forever seeking the language that sets our sights above
The rigmarole of life's duties and sometimes living rough
Developing a thick skin, even appearing a little tough

As we become acquainted with the softness abiding inside
Never from the world, our true selves can we hide
Oh shine our true real beauty, on such glory we can ride
Over all of life's boulders with surefootedness we do glide

¨♫♪ ♥ ♪♫*¨*

Magnificence

It's all a matter of trust
Between you and me and us
The only thing worthwhile
Is abiding in the world in this style

It's in the beauty of trust
That we relax and rely on us
In the essence of conviction
We experience any kind of liberation

All in the splendor of care
That we progress anywhere
Daring to live with true care
We're rare diamonds so very fair

¨♫♪ ♥ ♪♫*¨*

Shadows and Skies

I watch tree branches waving on the ground
Winds blowing shadows my eyes are bound
To absorb the movement, see this moment as a treat
Everything is transitory; we miss things when we blink

I watch tree shadows waving on the ground
My interest in such things, to some I astound
To be ever-present, I often close my eyes
Allowing my sight to go flying through mind's skies

¨♫♪ ♥ ♪♫*¨*

Awareness

Everything is moving under the infinite sky
Moving and zooming at a rate of knots
Time flies

Everything changes over land and in the sea
Per blink of the eye
Something new if we choose to see

Our lives are unfolding even they don't seem our own
Impersonal changing phenomenons
We grow and we grow

Embrace every moment
For all that it is
Awake, we'll never lose it
Awareness is bliss

¨♫♪ ♥ ♪♫*¨*

Drawn from Nature

Drawn from nature, inspiring art
Countless ways for us to impart
The message of our beating hearts
Every moment reveals somewhere to start

Carve from an ample experience of life
Fashion many moulds depicting life's spice
Carve the form lovingly, shape it long…
Communicate the beauty that has made you so strong

Invariably, the finished creation will encourage hearts to sing
Leading you to a new, enticing place to begin

¨♫♪ ♥ ♪♫*¨*

Our Roof

Consumed by the great, open sky
Its surrounding presence invokes us to feel high
Breathing sky in… one with all kin
Under the sky, we are living

In a moment, if ever feeling alone
Remember the sky is our canopy
Under which everyone is home

¨♫♪ ♥ ♪♫*¨*

Observations

Wind blowing through the trees
And, flickering on roadside ponds
Missing others in this life
Is akin to a heartfelt song

¨♫♪ ♥ ♪♫*¨*

Time Out

I am reducing my time staring into a computer screen
Looking out my window there is a rose blossoming to be seen
A pigeon pecking on grasses often overlooked
And, cockatoos squabbling over seeds getting off on the wrong foot

Leaves blowing in the breeze, so green and so lush
Flowing with the moment, no way in a rush
The sky clear and blue, I dive in with my mind
Into a world of imagination so great and sublime

I am reducing my time staring into a computer screen
Remembering my true nature, enabling my heart to beam
For too long I've forgotten the beauty of touch
So abundant in nature, like a true love crush

¨♫♪ ♥ ♪♫*¨*

On Life

Our lives are like white clouds floating by
Subtle changes occur in the blink of an eye
One moment an elephant, the next a bunnykin
Observing changing nature compels us to grin

And, then the clouds darken tumultuous and rough
When we're put to the test and life becomes tough
Here's an opportunity to grow and to learn
Understanding life's fluctuating nature lessens the burn

¨♫♪ ♥ ♪♫*¨*

Self Reveal

How to embody the goodness living inside?
Uncover the beauty glimmering ready to shine?
There are so many reasons to reveal our light to the world
Many very good reasons within every boy and girl
Our challenge is to believe in the love that's ours to give
Falling in love with our true Self is where it all begins…

¨♫♪ ♥ ♪♫*¨*

Freedom Jewels

Never give up
Believe with all heart
Manifest the reality we wish to impart
Upon the world, adorn beauty and pearls
Share liberating wisdom, offering freedom jewels

Never give up
Fill our thoughts with love
Our feelings are important
Worth all of the fuss
By generating loving kindness, gratitude too
Affects us all, not just a few

¨♫♪ ♥ ♪♫*¨*

We Are One

Sending you all my love
Despite feeling a little rough
Challenged to rise above
The grime, the grit, the sludge

Enduring the onslaught of living
Life's sufferings all around in no way forgiving
Each of us goes through anguish we are experiencing
What it means to be alive, what it means to be bringing in…

Peace, love, and light into the world
Although feeling pain, give love wings like a bird
Fly through dark clouds to clear skies feel the sun
Shower love on humanity, we are one

¨♫♪ ♥ ♪♫*¨*

Love's Grace

Elevate others
Elevate friends
Elevate all beings
Bridge hearts and mend
Around the corner to the other side
There is no bend where love can't abide
Gleaming and beaconing within every human's face
Ours for the showing
O holy love's grace

¨♫♪ ♥ ♪♫*¨*

Save Our Bees

Bees of pollination
Bees of grace
Without you what will humans face?
You are the queens of pure, dear nature
In essence you are our buzzing saviour

¨♫♪ ♥ ♪♫*¨*

Love Swell

Love is something so brand new
Yet it's old, imperfect, blemished too
Love is the comfy shoulder to rest on to renew
That warm, loving hand to hold so true

Love is our fur-family animals we so adore
It is the sunrise heralding a day ready to explore

Love is the air
Love is your friend
It's healing hearts yearning to mend

Love is beauty
Love is pain
A gathering of lessons in order to gain
Love our teacher, teaches us well
May our hearts ever grow in love and swell ...

¨♫♪ ♥ ♪♫*¨*

Love's Medicine Crop

Sending a hug to all dear friends
Holding you close, there is no end
To the perfect, true love abiding inside
Love living abundantly, no reason to hide

From its healing power, a plentiful fuel
So overflowing, into all hearts instil
Your own blend of brilliance
Love's medicine crop
We each form our own remedy
Love never stops

Lavish each other with all our love
Raise everyone up, lift love above

¨♫♪ ♥ ♪♫*¨*

Our Furry Friends

Our furry friends are very dear
We love them so much
People think we're queer

Doing everything to make them happy
It's doesn't matter people think we're whacky

Our furry friends keep us sane and whole
Providing for them is our goal
We bend, we beg, we love, we please
Our dear little friends intoxicate our hearts with ease

Thanks to the heavens for their love
Their very presence sends our hearts above
A soothing balm to the soul
Their being in our lives we do extol!

¨♫♪♥♪♫*¨*

Human Gold Mines

All around the world people are searching for gold
Gold-panning and mining
Extent of searching untold

When all around people are shining
Magnificence can't be sold
An invaluable significance
Hearts full of gold

A time will surely come when our worth will be seen
When humans know their beauty
Causing all souls to beam

Let's start with our essence glowing beneath our skin
Uncovering this is the true treasure uniting all kin

¨♫♪ ♥ ♪♫*¨*

Dona Nobis Pacem - Grant Us Peace

Grant us peace
Let's make a feast
To share lovingly across the land

Grant us peace
A peaceful feast
To absorb in our hearts
Peace so grand

Never bland
Oh, peaceful band
Love warriors making a stand

Always true
Knowing what to do
Peace filters through
Guiding our hands

Grant us peace
So life is a treat
Goodwill permeating all of man

Grant us peace
So we shall reap
Seeds sown to blossom …
Peace flourishes because peace can

¨♫♪ ♥ ♪♫*¨*

Sacred Qualities

Salute the sun glittering on the feathers of a bird
The beauty of a pleasant breeze
The warmth of another helping to make things better
A listening ear that bends with ease

Hail the hand that offers support
The heart that beats in love of your talk
The kindred spirit, blessed meeting of minds
Flying in time with one that understands your rhyme

Cherish the care of those who dare
Courage to care is really so rare
A sacred quality, we truly are one
May we elevate everyone under the sun

¨♫♪ ♥ ♪♫*¨*

We Are Miracles

Playing with miracles
Living our lives
Praise the Creative Source keeping us alive

Praise living beings
Exalt valuable life
On the wings of a miracle we all survive

We are a miracle
A glorious prayer
Soak up our sunshine
Breathe deeply the air

Consider ourselves miracles
Believe we're all suns
In our hearts shines a beauty
Global family, Precious Ones

¨♫♪ ♥ ♪♫*¨*

Dark of Night

Easier to discern
In the darkness of night
Is our light dim
Or do we beam bright?

¨♫♪ ♥ ♪♫*¨*

As One

One cell, one heart
All beings begin
From the same Mysterious Spark…

And, as life goes on..
We go about our ways…

It's a blessing whenever we share each other's days

¨♫♪ ♥ ♪♫*¨*

Love Floats

Sending love to everyone
Sending love to all
May this moment be good for you
May you experience the life you adore

It's in our reach to experience it
In doing so we don't need hands
Love lives in our hearts, it's established
When we live our love, we float over land

¨♫♪ ♥ ♪♫*¨*

The Friend's Song

Friends of love
Friends of grace
Soulful connections nothing can efface

Built from magic
Ties are strong
Facing all weather, friends get along

Stars in the day and the night
Inspiration personified, lights so bright

Uplifting beats we move along
Knowing the heart
And, soul of your song

¨♫♪ ♥ ♪♫*¨*

Promote Living

Take a rest when the workload is a test
A rest, a rest, removes all duress
For me writing a rhyme reduces any stress
In that I feel so very blessed

Doing what we love as often we can
Is a way to promote happy living on the land
When our work uplifts us, it's the ultimate fan
Cooling our days, walking along the seashore on smooth sand

¨♫♪ ♥ ♪♫*¨*

People Power

The potential of people power
When united, we can brilliantly flower
Permeating the essence of love
As one in the world, a peaceful dove

¨♫♪ ♥ ♪♫*¨*

Moments

A myriad of emotions going on around the world
In every man, woman, boy or girl
We are not alone in this living zone
Being compassionate and patient enables our hearts to atone

If we're not seeing clear, and we're been there before
Turn on the lights, open wide doors to explore
Step on in, release all shutters and sing
Every single moment is a new opportunity to begin

¨♫♪ ♥ ♪♫*¨*

Hail Life

Life is oh so brilliant
Colourful and remarkably resilient
Overcomes so many troubles
Like the phoenix rising from rubble

When in danger of losing hope
Hail opportunities to broaden one's scope
Sharpen the apparatus of the magnificent mind
Widen the heart to encompass humankind

¨♫♪ ♥ ♪♫*¨*

Sky Pie

Imagine tasting the brilliant, blue sky
Slices for everyone
Beautiful pie in the sky
Elevates our senses
Lifts us off the ground
Floating high above the earth
Wonder at the world so round

Imagine tasting the brilliant, blue sky
Limitless portions
Never goes to the thighs
Dissolves all defenses
Opens the eyes
Inseparable from nature,
No need for disguise

¨♫♪ ♥ ♪♫*¨*

Same Language

In the same language, everyone smiles
We communicate our heart's message
Body language style

A non-verbal message
Easy to perceive
Without opening one's mouth
A smile is clear to read

No need for articulation
The human smile is art
Unites us all
Reveals our divine spark

¨♫♪ ♥ ♪♫*¨*

Vision

Sometimes it's hard to see the Light
Despite its blinding magnificence
One must squint to see right

With all of life's challenges
Often involving pain
A slight adjustment in perception
Allows Light in again

¨♫♪ ♥ ♪♫*¨*

Great Sky

Clear blue, clear blue, clear blue, great sky
I imagine I dive into you, imagine I fly
Looking up into you
I envision a lullaby
Words written on your face
Soothing the heart's cry

¨♫♪ ♥ ♪♫*¨*

Melodies

The sound can deeply please
The music of the trees
Plays so gently on the breeze
Leaves blowing with grace and ease

Reminds that the time is ripe
Observing nature makes one bright
A heightened awareness will astound
And, keep feet softly on the ground

Breathing in the air, a gift so grand and fair
Inspires us to live and to give
Celebrate life with others, forthwith

The sound can deeply please
The music of the trees
May our tunes flow with such magnificent ease
Embodying the beauty of life-giving trees

¨♫♪ ♥ ♪♫*¨*

I Am Sky

Why is the sky so high?
I wish I could reach it
I wish I could fly
Combating gravity
Spreading my wings
Darting through clouds
What a way to live ...

Although the sky appears exceedingly high
I know through the air I breathe it
In essence I do fly
Gliding over seashores
Sailing above towns
In my imagination, I am buoyant
No need to land

¨♫♪ ♥ ♪♫*¨*

Remember

All of us are beautiful, all of us divine
The inherent magnificence of humankind
We simply don't remember, of course we forget
The precious baby that we once were
Full of wonder and no regret

Our mission is find ourselves hidden within
The innocent child, one with all kin
No comparisons, no judgement, no harsh words, no fight
Pure, gentle beauty, truth oh so right

I love you fellow human
We have been through so much
May life not be a struggle
Try not to rush…

¨♫♪ ♥ ♪♫*¨*

Human Sunshine

Sunshine ushers us to be okay
Seems to soothe our troubles away
Sends radiating brightness through the mind
Encourages us to feel better every time

Sunshine comes to save the day
A welcoming essence, there is no other way
To penetrate deeply into the bones so good
Uplifts and enlivens, benefits understood

Sunshine comes from your heart to mine
I love you fellow beings
Humans so kind

¨♫♪ ♥ ♪♫*¨*

Magnificent Sun

See the sun play on the land
Enticing us to feel magnificent and grand
Taking in light, we're uplifted and bright
Infused with a force to dazzle our nights

See the sun play on the land
Stretching arms wide, sun rays in our hands
Beacon in our heart, never depart
A haven of happiness, ours from the start

¨♫♪ ♥ ♪♫*¨*

Gold

The more we need to do
At the same time do less
Of the stress, the stress …
Causing us to digress

The more we need to do
Can make us feel blessed
Productivity is meditative
May be a considerable rest

Our actions are gold
The truth be told
Healthy activity
We'll never grow old

¨♫♪ ♥ ♪♫*¨*

Mind-Fields

Sitting in contemplation
In deep, deep thought
Sitting in contemplation
Musing over all I've been taught

Unlearning all that's not necessary
Confirming the treasures of worth
Letting go of the threads that can hamper me
Sowing love on lessons sprinkled with mirth

Our minds are a mind-field of goodness
The soil of happiness: our thoughts
Nurture the terrain with love-shine
Knowing that beyond our thoughts we're truly divine

¨♫♪ ♥ ♪♫*¨*

Long Live our Forests

Immersing oneself in nature is wonderful it's true
Experiencing the fullness of life exquisitely pouring through
Our very precious beings: our hearts, our lungs, our cells
The beauty of our beings surely and vastly excels

Intoxicating to take so many deep breaths
Among so many trees, we feel like a guest
Having no need to wear our finest best
All that matters is that we burst with great zest

Inhaling the beauty of a forest is real
A splendour so nourishing and tangible to feel
Drinking in the sights; becoming one with tree-kin
In search of life's essence, this is where to begin …

Immersing oneself in nature is wonderful it's true
Long live our forests: let's nurture them too!

¨♫♪ ♥ ♪♫*¨*

See in the Night

I surrender to love
I surrender to life
Lay down my arms to worldly strife

Instead of worry, may I harness the courage?
To take action to remove any luggage
Of fearing and being in a helpless state
When nothing comes good if my own self I berate

Determined to love
Only action depends
May I follow my heart and see where the path lends

Outcome to the journey:
Joy and light
Open my eyes to see in the night

¨♫♪♥♪♫*¨*

Breathing Brilliance

Make these breaths count
It's what life is all about
Breathe them in
Breathe them out

Slowly
Deeply
Down inside
Fill the body
With what makes us alive

Make no haste
To breathe back in
Observe tingles on the skin

Then exhale
The great release
Be there present
This moment's a treat

The breathing brilliance
Sweet mechanism
A living system
Embraces all kin

Breathing bodies
Full of light
Our souls unite us
Hearts alight

¨♫♪ ♥ ♪♫*¨*

Dear Kin

I am searching in the great sky
For a thread, a fragment, upon which to rely
To heal me, uplift me, fill me with love
Encompass me with ability to enable me to rise above
Life's daily hurdles that could even trip a dove
The battlefield of learning about our humanness is sometimes tough

When fragility is a weakness, vulnerability perceived as sin
The truth of life's suffering inherently affects us all Dear Kin

Whatever the circumstance, take a breath, contemplate the Light
Shine it on others, be beacons in the night
Empathy, understanding is the medicine from where to begin
We are in life's journey together
Let our fashion be about making hearts sing

¨♫♪ ♥ ♪♫*¨*

Sun Pool

I'm the sparkling sun
Creating a pool on the ground
A shining piece of light
To disappear I am bound …

¨♫♪ ♥ ♪♫*¨*

Beauty Spot

Do you see me sitting here perched in the trees?
Do you see me without a care, obscured by branches and leaves?
I am a pigeon with multi-coloured feathers; I fly with grace and ease
I'm a pigeon that weathers all weather, I move wherever I please

Do you see me resting here wings outstretched on the bush?
Magnificent wings dotted with life, I'm worth a second look
I am a moth with a golden coat, I flutter when I fly
I'm a moth that loves the light, and I'm pleasing to the eye

Do we see nature in its many forms that makes us gasp and sigh?
Do we see Her beauty everyday, mysterious magic on display?
The beauty within us is also oh so good; we're a brilliant, shining lot
Reflected all around, when we open our eyes: beauty in every spot

¨♫♪ ♥ ♪♫*¨*

Sparkling Coat

The sun shines on the magnificent sea
A glistening, sparkling coat to see
Covers her form in a moving way
Shimmers, glitters: takes your breath away

Observing the magic of nature's displays
Entranced by the spectacle changing every day
'Same, same but different'
God's mystery is good
Through the glory of nature, divinity is understood

¨♫♪ ♥ ♪♫*¨*

Peace: The Universal Hood

Peace I see reflected back at me
In the eyes of humans without disguise
People that bear their hearts and their souls
Devoted to sharing loving-kindness
Compassion, the goal

Peace I see in the land and sea
Looking with eyes loving creativity
Relishing the sights, celebrating the love
With the joy of a child
We live life above

Beyond the oceans, beyond the clouds
Peace is everywhere to be found
Living inside of us, peace lifts us up
Sharing it with others fills everyone's cup

Uncover our peace and spread it around
Permeate its essence all over town
And, throughout the world
Oh so good
Peace within is the universal hood

¨♫♪ ♥ ♪♫*¨*

The Butterflies' Buzz

Beautiful butterflies abound in the air
Their exquisite presence reduces despair
Fluttering wings beauty shimmering light
The affect of their allure is quite out of sight

Permeating magic: it's the butterflies' buzz
Our part is to keep nature beautiful
And, She'll look after us

¨♫♪ ♥ ♪♫*¨*

Peaceful Ocean

The sound is ever-constant
Circles through our minds
Chatter so incessant
Self-dialogue fine or blows your mind

Do we follow the inner conversation… ceaselessly leading on?
Or do we watch it unfolding, contemplating from where it comes from?

Observing without attaching, to our thoughts is the peaceful way
Non-reaction depletes emotions that often lead us astray

Our true self resides beyond the commotion, of riding our busy minds
Our true self is like an ever-flowing ocean, deep and sublime and bright

¨♫♪ ♥ ♪♫*¨*

Sky Writers

The wind blows
Materials flow
With a gust out of the trees

Somewhat lighter
Trees stand brighter
Loose strands now gone with the breeze

Goodbye feathers and stray blossoms
Shreds of bark on a new journey embarks
And, forgetting not the spiralling leaves
Writing in the sky
Pens playing an important part

¨♫♪ ♥ ♪♫*¨*

Our Teachers

Trees breathe and show the way
Branches point, move and sway
Riding the weather, bearing the storm
Look to them when we feel forlorn

Representing strength
Upright ease
How do they endure as if life's a breeze?
Roots deeply embedded in the ground
Yet, on their trunks scars can be found

Trees weather the sleet and the sun
Climatic fluctuations would not be fun
Exposed to the elements, oh trees are good
We have so much to learn from them, if only we would …

¨♫♪ ♥ ♪♫*¨*

Manifestation

I focus on my vision
This sight will see me through
Never detract from my goal
Rise complete and new

I throw off any division
Harmful shreds of doubt
Any shadow of negation
I can surely live without

I focus on my vision
This sight will see me through
My intention is my destination
I trust in the process too

¨♫♪ ♥ ♪♫*¨*

Believe

He told me to believe, my dear friend Swamiji
With my entire mind believe
Trust, dream big, and perceive

The reality of my thoughts manifest
Let my body do the rest
Reveal the workings of my mind
The body is the apparatus that chimes the mind's rhyme

One day it never comes, only *today* exists for us
'I am' as opposed to 'I will'
Infuse faith to help me instil
The actuality that I esteem
Living the life of my dreams
In reach if only I truly believe
Trust my mind to unlock the key

¨♫♪ ♥ ♪♫*¨*

Ways of Life

Lessons can be found in the air
Clouds are teachers floating up there
Displaying the penetrating truth of life
Everything changes, impermanence is rife

Here one moment, gone the next
That cloud-shaped dragon could never cause any vex
Disappears into sheer, blue sky
Leaving our thoughts to wonder why …

Life is so transient
Amazing too
Affects us all, not just a few
We're all in this together
In the ways of life
May we love each other and cause no strife

¨♫♪♥♪♫*¨*

Observe

Celebrate love, celebrate care
Celebrate the uplifting element of air
Pure to breath, oxygen is life
Polluting its quality causes untold strife

Celebrate foundations, celebrate earth
Celebrate the core of grounding worth
An abundant mother giving mirth
Dismissing her generosity: nothing could be worse

Celebrate water, celebrate joy
Celebrate all molecules of emotion to enjoy
Water has memory, water is mind
Compromising its source is a shame on humankind

¨♫♪ ♥ ♪♫*¨*

Two Trees

Do they see us standing here swaying in the breeze?
Do they notice us holding hands, branches entwined with air and ease?
We're two trees without a care; our duty is to flow…
Breathing on beings everywhere, enabling life to grow

¨♫♪ ♥ ♪♫*¨*

In-sight

Stop for a moment
Watch your breath
Observe it riding so effortless

Feel it rising
Witness its fall
Guiding you through a hidden door

Into the unknown
The breath is a bridge
Between two worlds
Knowing this is bliss

The seen and unseen
Two worlds unite
In closing our eyes
We gain insight

¨♫♪ ♥ ♪♫*¨*

Living Giving Love

Oh Dear Friends when we experience pain
May we relax any vex to keep things sane
Being there for each other shows we care
Extending our hearts is love's true flair
Time has come to shine the light
Living giving love
A human's right

¨♫♪ ♥ ♪♫*¨*

Glisten

'How can life be more beautiful?'
Said the dewdrop to the sky.
'I know how to make it more beautiful…
I'll glisten like a colourful eye'

¨♫♪ ♥ ♪♫*¨*

Oh Butterfly

Oh butterfly flying sweetly by
Fluttering about your ways
Your life is very precious
Your days are so few
Reminding us of our beauty
Colourful and transient too

¨♫♪ ♥ ♪♫*¨*

The Prize

Giving up is not an option
Failure is defeat
Letting go of your efforts is not the solution
Neither is working for some small treat

May our determination be irrepressible
May our sight penetrate beyond the skies
Dismiss all doubts and narrow speculations
Your heart on the goal is really the prize

¨♫♪ ♥ ♪♫*¨*

Reunions

Visiting friends who are a blast from the past
Souls-uplift, feelings unsurpassed
Hearts relax, we take a breath
Oh so comfortable with our old, brand new guest

¨♫♪ ♥ ♪♫*¨*

Beacons

Spread your sunshine on a cloudy day
Infuse greater light when everything's grey
And, cold, and old, and falling away
Enhance the atmosphere with our own sunny ray

Things are never so bleak when reaching within
The love and light inside can make ourselves grin
From ear to ear, our radiance lights the world
We're human beacons, a beauty to behold

¨♫♪ ♥ ♪♫*¨*

Abundant Gifts

The Universe provides
In immeasurable colourful disguise
The vehicle for salvation
Materialises to offer satiation

We never know how they will appear
Expressions of creation
Prompting us to steer
Gifts abundantly given to us
Oh Dear Nature in you we trust!

¨♫♪ ♥ ♪♫*¨*

Sacred Sparks

I'm inspired to write a poem to set my mind free
Compelled to pen a beauty filled with love and liberty
Poetry is a rest from working at my best
A wonderful release, causing me to feel blessed

So thank you from my heart
For sharing the message I impart
Thank you for cherishing
Our divine and sacred sparks

¨♫♪ ♥ ♪♫*¨*

One Love

One love in the world is what we are
Beaming magnificence, brilliance, we're all superstars
Inspiring others, enriching lives
The love inside us bursts beyond disguise

When we're there for each other
We open up
Overflowing, yes, we fill everyone's cup
Love is limitless, it knows no bounds
An unconditional capacity to traverse every land

One love in this world is what we are
Activate your radiance and spread love's magic far

¨♫♪ ♥ ♪♫*¨*

Grasp It

'Since it is all too clear
It takes time to grasp it'

Because our minds guide and steer
Enlightening truths may surpass us

We need some time to absorb the light
Radiating evidence shining in the night

Blinked thinking keeps facts thin
When always true clarity beckons us in

Meditating on moments works a treat
Looking within for all we seek
Liberating insights, the fruits we reap
In contemplation our hearts can truly speak

¨♫♪♥♪♫*¨*

Giving

'Before receiving
There must be giving' ~ *Lao-tzu*

Before receiving
There must be giving
Celebrate the cycle of life

Accompanying conceiving
Is believing
Imagination filled with light

More blissful to give than to receive
Filling hearts brings us joy
So blissful to love and set hearts at ease
Potent perfume permeates the sky

¨♫♪ ♥ ♪♫*¨*

Sparkle

I think you are magic
It's true I think you are
The essence of you is magic
Shine on oh bright star

Your love light beams with brilliance
Sparkling near and far
Your kind self is truly brimming
With love and light, this you are

¨♫♪ ♥ ♪♫*¨*

Gliding High

Gloriously gliding
Birds flying by
See how they gracefully cross the sky

Gloriously gliding
Birds flying by
The quiet from observing
Makes me feel high

¨♫♪ ♥ ♪♫*¨*

Breathe the Breeze

Taking the moment to breathe the breeze
Invigorates our aura, our mind's at ease
Our hearts take rest, we're very blessed
In this kingdom where we are guests

Taking the moment to breathe the breeze
Tantalises inspiration, our spirits are pleased
Where 'Guest is God', we penetrate fog
Oh yes we can jump over any log

¨♫♪ ♥ ♪♫*¨*

Our Every Step

'Wheresoever you go, go with all your heart' ~ *Confucius*

Wheresoever you go
Go with all your heart
Wherever your heart shall flow
A brilliant radiance may you bestow

Upon your every moment
On all beings living within
The beauty of the present
It's shining, beckoning us to sing

Of the wonders of creation
The beating of our hearts
Magnificent, marvellous celebrations
So many reasons to impart

Joy in our every step
A kick within our beat
Share the beauty of our breath
With everyone we meet

¨♫♪ ♥ ♪♫*¨*

Permeate

'Real love begins when nothing is expected in return'
~ Antoine de Saint-Exupéruy

When free-flowing giving is receiving
True love is what we earn
Real love is when nothing is expected
We learn, we live, and we turn

Good-tidings ever-growing
We sow the seeds of joy
Loving that's giving is singing
Hearts wider than the sky

Infusing our every action
Imbued with loving light
Love is a one-way action
Permeating you and I

¨♫♪ ♥ ♪♫*¨*

Meaning

A poem of love
A poem of joy
Encouraging good actions
To employ
Every measure we can muster
We can make
May our every breath be cause to celebrate

The manifestations of our day-to-day
Creating our lives in our own special way
Fulfilling our purpose, our duties, our lot
Realising we ultimately write our own plot

Take on this moment with all that it brings
Even if it means kick-starting to sing
There's meaning in the madness
There's meaning there is
Discovering answers
Is every reason to live

¨♫♪ ♥ ♪♫*¨*

Mystery Guest

The sun visits from outer space
Shining its rays upon my face
Warming the earth
Growing flowers
Cultivating the land with its magical powers

Oh how we hail our mystery guest
A gift from the heavens
Our flourishing success
On which our lives thrill and survive
A guiding star keeping us alive

¨♫♪ ♥ ♪♫*¨*

Ever-Evolving

When you get to the top of the mountain, keep climbing ~ Zen proverb

When you get to the top of the mountain
Keep climbing
Never stop
When you arrive at the top of the mountain
It's only the beginning
Another step to an unseeable top

Keep climbing beyond the stratosphere
Of your mind and into the stars
Continue exploring the expanse of the Universe
Visit planets, shed light on the dark

Our journey is ever-unfolding
Achievements are only to gain
A foot-hold to the next moment
Our lives ever-evolving, never the same

¨♫♪ ♥ ♪♫*¨*

Our Words

We reveal our mind
When we speak unkind
Darkened thoughts not worth holding on to

Question their essence
Their pretence and presence
Emitting a consequence diffused from divine

All that we say
Our hearts do portray
Is it light or dark we wish to convey?

The state of our health
Lies in our mind's great wealth
Let us speak words that brighten the day

¨♫♪ ♥ ♪♫*¨*

Dear Everyone

Hello Dear Everyone
It's a new day
Wishing you love
And, good spirits in every way

No matter where we are
We're connected in kind
No one is separate
We are One and Divine

This life is our challenge
To see through the dark
Find the light within
Shine our love spark

Our mission to keep going
And, never give up
A journey we're taking
Each day a new start

Sincere cheer to Everyone
It's a new day
Wishing great love
Sending big hugs your way

¨♫♪ ♥ ♪♫*¨*

Divine It

'Develop the mind of equilibrium. You will always be getting praise and blame, but do not let either affect the poise of the mind: follow the calmness, the absence of pride.' ~Buddha

The beauty of balance
Sweet equipoise
Denotes refinement of the mind

We seek to divine it
To explore
The mystery of humankind's mind

This can only be done within oneself
Unlocking ourselves; we unlock the world

Mastering ourselves we uncover truth pearls
Living insides us all of the time

¨♫♪ ♥ ♪♫*¨*

The Source

'One's source is within oneself. Give yourself up to it. That means that you should seek the source and merge with it' ~ *Ramana Maharshi*

Our source is within us
We are never without
The essence inside us
Its power could knock us out

One glimpse within
Inspires our hearts to sing
Merging with true beauty
Elevates all kin

Give ourselves up to the soft knocking at our door
Perceive the inner calling beseeching one to explore
The human, the heart, life's meaning, and light
Hear the gentle whispering of your heart through the night

By seeking our source we fuse and beam bright
Uplifting our existence embracing life's flight

¨♫♪ ♥ ♪♫*¨*

Field of Life

Welcome to the playground of my mind
To gather here our hearts will bind
A visit oh so potentially divine
Sublime, we chime, in time, we rhyme

In the arena of the precious mind
There are no limits
There are no blights
Creating our realities as we wish
Ultimately, life manifests as we see fit

The mind is fertile
Profusely ripe
Luscious soil to sow good light
Tending to mind's flowers, watch them grow
In the field of life, let's shine and glow

¨♫♪ ♥ ♪♫*¨*

Patience

Patience is a virtue
Patience is divine
An endearing quality
Soothes the mind

Manifesting this behaviour
Is such a victory
A redeeming feature
Ensures one's sanity

All of us have it
Patience that sets us free
Its essence empowers us
Serenity is liberty

¨♫♪ ♥ ♪♫*¨*

Alive

Feel the beating of your heart
What are the emotions you wish to impart?
To express feelings in words is what sets us apart
In verbal communication humans can embark

Animals express in many other ways
The angst of their hearts when their babies go astray
Desperation of their calls, endless searching in the eyes
Encoded with the care of nature, humans aren't the only ones to cry

Never dismiss nature's subtle messages
In observing its language our perception grows
We're really not so different, we strive to live and survive
We're really not so different; it's a blessing to be alive

¨♫♪ ♥ ♪♫*¨*

Creative Touch

Something creative
Something good
An artful something to be understood
Delve into your memory
Explore your heart
Express that something you wish to impart

All of us are poets
Articulating our own ways
At times, all of us like to stargaze
What makes your heart sings?
Share with us
Your unique vibrations
Creative touch

¨♫♪ ♥ ♪♫*¨*

Little Sea Urchin

Little Sea Urchin
Where did you go?
You've left us your body
Beautiful shell in the flow

The memory of your presence
Has a sacred glow
Teaching us of impermanence
And from this we grow

Into wiser beings
Because all things must pass
May we make the most of each moment
As if it's the last

¨♫♪ ♥ ♪♫*¨*

Magical Mysteries

Words are wonderful
When they're true
Dressing the thoughts of the inner you

Expressing the heart
Oh, words they care
To sing of peace and love to share

Words are powerful
They mean so much
Reaching beyond the physical touch

Communication bridges
Over all the world's shores
Magical mysteries, to be sure

¨♫♪ ♥ ♪♫*¨*

Oneness In Love

Oneness in Love
Elevates the skies above
Unifying all hearts and minds

The air we breathe flows through you and me
Embraces our beings supremely sublime

Ultimately inseparable
Our spirits are indelible
The essential truth of souls is divine

If we really knew the power
Profound delicate human flowers
We'd create reality for all of us to shine

¨♫♪ ♥ ♪♫*¨*

Peaceful PathWay

A peaceful pathway
Infused with light
And, beauty
Flowers
Love so bright

Its essence beckons us to no end
All about the journey
Our life and friends

A peaceful pathway
May we track
Leaving no fires
From deeds we enact

Building bridges
Smooth the way
For each other
Make a happier day

Intrinsically linked
You and me
Our peaceful pathway is full of discovery
Take precious time to smell the roses
Contemplate mysteries this life poses

¨♫♪ ♥ ♪♫*¨*

Live and Sleep Fully

May everyone sleep well tonight
Rest our heads
Forget any blights
Run with the angels
Energetic, upright
Independent and stable
Functioning right

May everyone waken with spirits strengthened
Encouraged to merge with our kin and our friends
Face the new day with an upbeat attitude
Living our lives to an inspiring tune

¨♫♪ ♥ ♪♫*¨*

Living True

Bridging family and friends...

New beginnings
Heaven-sent
Forgive past troubles
Ensure time well-spent

Embrace good vibes
Create fresh tunes
Life on earth ends all too soon

Look beyond deeds mis-done
Everyone errs under the sun
Takes forgiveness to start anew
Feel deeply your heart
Living true

¨♫♪ ♥ ♪♫*¨*

The mind at home in our hearts

How to quieten the mind, the mind?
And, elevate to a wider dimension
How to express our heart and soul?
Beyond the standard convention

In communicating oneself in restricted verse
The accepted means applied today
In conveying one's worth, trying to find mirth
What are the ways we can portray?

The essence of our feelings
The profound core of our being
That's what is needed today
To quieten the mind and hear our hearts sing
Be inspired in our own unique way

Uncover hidden sparks
Our creative spirit
Results in ever-widening joy
A calm and imaginative mind enables love to deliver us
Finding home within our hearts

¨♫♪ ♥ ♪♫*¨*

Friends

True friends will be there in the end
No matter life's spins and bends
Have the capacity to see colour in grey
Strength to survive difficult days

Hearts beat through thick and thin
Wonderful how it is with life's good kin
Despite the expanse of time apart
Always ready to make a new start

True friends will be there in the end
Blissful, God-Blessed, Heaven-sent
Invaluable gifts their presence brings
Being with friends is time well-spent

¨♫♪ ♥ ♪♫*¨*

Peaceful, Precious Freedom

'You can't separate peace from freedom because no one can be at peace unless he has his freedom.' ~ Malcolm X

Freedom and Peace are inseparable brothers
Joined by the heart
Living, breathing beloveds

Intrinsic existence
Impossible without the other
Peace that's free
Needs no division, no borders

No nationalities: no yours and no mine
All of us families
Under the one sun we shine

¨♫♪ ♥ ♪♫*¨*

Wholeness

Inspired by Chapter 22 of the Tao The Ching, Lao Tzu

'Bend and you will remain whole'
Be unassuming and you will excel
By being empty, we will always be filled
Growing old, is to be renewed

Having little is to gain
Material surplus is in truth, weight
No need to justify, and one is known
No need to boast of ability, then one is shown

The essence of success is to endure
Competing with no one, no one competes with you
Curl like the Willow to be straight
Attaining wholeness is cause to celebrate

¨♫♪ ♥ ♪♫*¨*

Selfless Sea

Is it not because he is selfless
That his Self is realised? ~ Tao Teh Ching, Lao Tzu

By selfless deeds we find ourselves
The greater Self flowing through you and me
Through thinking of others
Understanding our oneness with brothers
Such truths do set us free

When giving recovers
Healing from suffering under covers
Reach out your heart and hand

No stranger lives inside you
In essence we are brand new
Life's great mystery in every land

Accomplish selfless deeds as the one true feat
Reasons for living in this world

Make it the benchmark
The heart of us to impart
Create beauty from your Selfless Sea

¨♫♪ ♥ ♪♫*¨*

Be Still

Translation of Tao Teh Ching ~ Verse 47
Affirmation ~ By staying still, I am aware of more...

Know the ways of the world
Without walking out of the door
See the Way of Heaven
Without looking through the window

Stay still
To know more

The wise know without travelling
Has insight without looking
Manifests without effort

¨♫♪ ♥ ♪♫*¨*

Mystical Wholeness

Translation of Verse 56 of Tao Teh Ching ~ Lao Tzu

'Still waters run deep'
When one knows one does not speak

'Empty vessels make the most noise'
He who speaks does not know

To unite the world into one whole
Despite this seeming an impossible goal
When doing less achieves more
Block all passages
Shut the door

In effort to harmonise all lights
Blunt sharp edges
Untangle all ties

Bonding the world into a Mystical Whole
Begs no effort, or nothing to turn from
No benefit or no harm shall bring
No honour or need for humbling

¨♫♪ ♥ ♪♫*¨*

Embrace Growth

I bow to this moment
And all that it brings
I bow to the lessons
Learning teaches me to sing

I grow as a consequence
Growing keeps me alive
I flow with new reverence
What it means to survive

The down times
The doldrums
Days in the rough
When things don't go smoothly
And, happiness you bluff

Keeping our heads above water
Let's ride all life's waves
Another new day taller
Embrace growth everyday

¨♫♪ ♥ ♪♫*¨*

Only Love can do That (World of Brightened Skies)

'I will mourn the loss of thousands of precious lives, but I will not rejoice in the death of one, not even an enemy. Returning hate for hate multiplies hate, adding deeper darkness to a night already devoid of stars. Darkness cannot drive out darkness: only light can do that. Hate cannot drive out hate, only love can do that.' ~ Martin Luther King, Jr

Oh, Martin Luther King
You were so wise
Even now so many good folk don't realise
The profundity of your embracing words
Your love of humanity, if only more heard

Mourning for thousands of precious lost lives
A commendable task of the soul-realised
Refraining from rejoicing in the death of one
Is truly great, even if an enemy on the run

Returning hate for hate
Deepens the darkness of starless nights
Darkness strengthens hate
Only Light can turn on the Light

Hate cannot banish hate
Only love can claim the prize
Of humans living in peace
Within a world of brightened skies

¨♫♪ ♥ ♪♫*¨*

Soar

~ Artwork by my Mum

Consider this moment as it is
The gift of life's presence
Of all it brings

Packed with experiences
Oh, life she lives
Bursting with action
Inviting us to give

Energy to our everyday
Creating a difference
An invaluable way
To elevate consciousness
Raise the bar
Make known the unknown
Wherever you are

Consider this moment as it is
Explore life's shores
Your inner star
Take up the challenge to shine your light
It's never too dark when burning bright

Life is an adventure
Destination unknown
Beam light on your journey
Everywhere is home

This moment is a blessing
Relish it galore
Oh Dear Life, see me soar

¨♫♪ ♥ ♪♫*¨*

Our Essence

~ Artwork by my Mum

I wish I were a flower
Blowing in the breeze with nature's power
Permeating perfume through my surrounds
Shining beauty all over town

I wish I were a butterfly
A flying flower across the sky
Magnificent colours flashing by
Abundant beauty giving you a high

However, I am thankful I'm a human
All colours of the rainbow run right through me
To be anything else would be a tragedy
The essence of humanity is full of grace and majesty

¨♫♪ ♥ ♪♫*¨*

Born with Wings

'You were born with wings....
Why prefer to crawl through life?" ~ Rumi

Born with wings
But forgotten how to fly
Born with the ability to soar sky high
Yet, somehow, somewhere
Lost the inspiration to try

Crawling upon the ground
See the earth up close
Crawling on the ground
When flying would benefit us most

Spread your heart wide
Elevate the mind
Cultivate spiritual foods to prevent any nose dives

Transcend all barriers that keep you weighted down
Alleviate dimensions that may bring about one's frown
Navigate the sky ways to sustain you on your course
Levitate to fine ways celebrating our Divine Source

¨♫♪ ♥ ♪♫*¨*

The Ultimate Gift

Nature hasn't got a human heart
The wisdom of this message helps me start
To see the error of emotional haze
The depth of my attachment
Wanting my animals to stay

But, animals are inherently wise
Moving through life without a disguise
Questioning not, they take life on
And, when it's time to go
Animals prove so strong

An innate intelligence
Guides their way
They don't grieve in tune with human dismay
Reminding us of the strife of life
When we demand permanence, we turn off a light

To the truth of existence
And of all our kin
Each moment is a blessing
We live therein
Change is upon us with every breath
Embracing this flux is such a gift

Nature hasn't got a human heart
Thinking rationally is a very good start
To reduce the emotion, deduct the haze
Adopt the inclination to live full days

Then let go with all your heart
Observe living and dying on its great flight
Two sides of the same coin
Life and death is
Accepting this is the Ultimate Gift

¨♫♪ ♥ ♪♫*¨*

Elevated Heights

We all lose someone so sweet
At times in our lives, this sadness we'll meet
It's part of the joy and all of the love
The depth of our sadness
Shows how our hearts floated above

We all lose someone so sweet
It's an unavoidable fact
Not something we greet

The time to say goodbye
Often makes us cry
Breaks our hearts feeling we too will die

Reminds us to remember that *all things must pass*
No one gets out alive
From this life we eventually surpass

Moving beyond the world's pastures
Onto a greater flight
Promoting us, one hopes, to elevated heights

¨♫♪ ♥ ♪♫*¨*

We Are Forever

We think Forever
Because *we are* Forever
Beyond the cycle of life

Our spirits are Forever
And, love lives Forever
Taking it with us on all flights

Awareness goes with us
Developed inside us
Cannot be taken away

Love and Compassion
All heart's salvation
Goodness never leads us astray

We think Forever
And, we love each other
Never wishing to part

When we let go of attachment
Trusting all things are meant
Surrendering to the Divine creates a happier day

¨♫♪ ♥ ♪♫*¨*

Master Mind

The mind is everything; what you think you become ~ Buddha

The mind is everything
You become what you think

The mind is everything
If you don't know this, you could possibly sink

Into deep depression
Moody and glum
Being around you, no idea of fun

The mind is your master
Driving the bus
Be careful about what causes you to fuss

Is it worth unbalancing your mind?
Observe its workings
Never become unkind

Your actions are precious
Your vibrations gold
Let us live mindfully before growing cold

¨♫♪ ♥ ♪♫*¨*

'Know Thyself'

Knowing Thyself
Is so easy to say
Harder to implement in any real way

Conditioned with beliefs
Beyond our own mind
Genetic imprints are sometimes not kind

On the Core Level
Soul Level too
Underlying Beliefs can lead us askew
And, the History Level needs to be resolved
Before becoming too, too old

'Know Thyself'
Wise Socrates did say
Take care of yourself come what may

Elevate our lives
Look within
Take every action
Let your heart sing

"♫♪ ♥ ♪♫*"*

Resilient You

How do you go on when your energy is low?
I don't know; just go with the flow
Of life's punches and all they bring
You never know from them you might sing

About the fruits of your pains and of all you gain
Preserving despite the effort until you drain
Every morsel of your endurance and strength
Stretching your neck out and going to great lengths

To meet the needs, rise above
Living in harmony with events like a dove
Surprising yourself: meet your Truth
Resilience lives inside gold and good

¨♫♪ ♥ ♪♫*¨*

Us

The power of our words is exceptional
Our thoughts create our reality and *it is so*
To be master of our minds instigates the flow
Of how we wish to live and completely grow

Generate good love for everyone; send goodwill to all beings under the sun
Look around and see the beauty of above, shines so strongly within
Mirroring you Beautiful Love Dove

¨♫♪ ♥ ♪♫*¨*

Oneness

All embracing oneness in our hearts let's never forget
The bridging of each other in every part: it's heaven sent
So very hard to believe we're all divine most never met
Pays us to remember we're on voyage that's kismet

Human character is the hardest to change, we know, isn't it
Our true natures hidden inside, to reveal it is a feat
Most of us are too shy to shine our exquisite, blinding light
Most of us rather decry our love, and live life tough

Let's shed our skins and walk within the oneness of our flight
Humans trying to survive, sharing life with all our rights
When we see our brothers and sisters experiencing hardships full of blight
Take the opportunity to do the best, caring for humans with all our might

¨♫♪ ♥ ♪♫*¨*

Share Good Medicine

Healing is such a powerful thing
Making our essence sing and grin
With so much beauty
Love divine
A gracious gift for humankind

It's in our potential
And so essential
To empower our being
With health we're meant for

Embodies our life
Inspires the spice
Carrying us through hard days and nights

Provides the reason
In every season
Uplifts our hearts
To dismiss any treason
From those who have forgotten the love
Forgotten how to love, finding it tough

We all are healers in our own way
Each has our own medicine to save the day
Sprinkle it everywhere far and wide
From love may no one run and hide

¨♫♪ ♥ ♪♫*¨*

Giving Sunshine

A beautiful poem written with love
Elevates the skies above
And in our mind
Feelings trigger sublime
Celebrating mysterious humankind

A poem bridges hearts so true
The heart beating inside you
Enlivens more love, more flair to care
Extend your warm hand to those in despair

Create this moment as you wish
Consider who you'd like to share it with
All the sunshine, golden joy
Give it to others, love's brand new toy

¨♫♪ ♥ ♪♫*¨*

World in Love

The day we fall in love with ourselves
Is the day the world will be free
Acknowledging and knowing the beauty of our creation
Incites within us every cause for celebration

Peace must reign within our hearts
Before we see it around us
Its essence comes from inside first
Judgement of others is no delegation

The World in Love
Filled with people in love
Would be so very dear
To live and give in the beauty of divine love
In this way our lives must be steered

¨♫♪ ♥ ♪♫*¨*

Brave Souls

You are so brave
How can it be?
To live life without amenities
Without warm shelters
Without warm beds
I admire your brave souls
Living improperly fed

Taking my hat off to you
I give you mine
Brother, sister
Souls so fine
I care for you
We are as One
Our lives linked
With Everyone

¨♫♪ ♥ ♪♫*¨*

Empathetic Action

Empathetic Action
Needed for people who live tough
Existing on the streets without shelter
Enduring life so rough

Our homeless family submitted to society's bluff
Today's throw away attitude
Must have luxuries and stuff

Indispensable people
Lives a strew
How could we ever forget you?
Going without, so some can live large
Whoever knew you're our real stars

But this can't go on
The truth must be seen
It's in our hands to create a new scene
Waking from sad dreams
Let's open the way
For a brighter, happier, healthier new day

¨♫♪ ♥ ♪♫*¨*

United

Our lives are nothing
If not each others
Intrinsically linked
Shared with brothers

Our breaths are bridges
To one and all
United in living
United in a fall

It's our responsibility
To see when we're down
For our human family we must make a stand
Never turning away
We strike the light
Rekindle hope to us living out at night

Build new homes to take us in
House and feed our living kin
With so much love
We will construct new lives
Valued family, the future's bright

¨♫♪ ♥ ♪♫*¨*

May love come knocking

Life goes on around you
When you don't go out
When you must remain at home
With a physical challenge or something like that

Many things start anew
Events, activities, things people do
Seasons come and then they go
Without really including or missing you

It could tip you over life's very edge
The push would come from a very strong pledge
To give up on the moment and what it brings
When refusing to see the simple things

That make our lives
It's not all sugar and spice
The uneventful moments can really be nice
We must relax in them despite it all
Trust in love that knocks on the door

¨♫♪ ♥ ♪♫*¨*

Revealing our Inner Star

Everything works out in the end
Even if things drive you round the bend
Take deep breaths
Dig down deep
Trust that inside lay the answers you seek

Everything works out when you share with friends
The beauty of your silence when you visit them
Thinking aloud your friend just knows
What lives in your heart, how you grow

Trust in others beyond yourself
We are here for each other, the problem's solved
A problem shared is a problem halved
In revealing ourselves shines our inner star

¨♫♪ ♥ ♪♫*¨*

Rise Above

'If you are irritated by every rub, how will you be polished?'
~ Rumi

When every little itch causes us to scratch
When life's simple rub imbues a rash
A tiny jolt may cause us to dash
Then life truly seems a difficult bash

Why oh why do our petals easily fall?
When we are so precious
Knocking to the floor
Every effort we have mustered, we have made
To be strong and tough in life's parade

Strengthen up and lengthen our stride
Take each blunder with inner pride
We are so strong
Our spirits are a song
Beyond the touch of all earthly wrongs

¨♫♪ ♥ ♪♫*¨*

Our Merciful Capacity

It only takes a moment to pen a poem singing and swimming in love
It only takes a moment of loving
To lift oneself above

The trials and tribulations of this life
The let downs and living rough
The disappointments and the blues
The people who call your bluff

It only takes a moment to right the wrongs we may have done
People are so very forgiving
Living in the light of the sun

If it only takes a moment to recognise love's glorious light
Open our eyes to see with clarity
The merciful capacity of human might

¨♫♪ ♥ ♪♫*¨*

Set Heaven Free

To love each other is what we're here to do
To care, caress, to love each other true
Every human being needs to know love
Set the kingdom of heaven free in our hearts like a dove

¨♫♪ ♥ ♪♫*¨*

Beautiful Wings

Beauty is as beauty does
Beautiful actions
Defines hearts of a dove

Clear to perceive
Beautiful wings
They caress the heart
With a heady blend

A golden hue
Upon your crown
Beautiful actions
Uplifts the whole town

Inside out
True beauty is deep
Look within
For the truth we seek

¨♫♪ ♥ ♪♫*¨*

The Perfect Prayer

Penning poetry is the perfect prayer
To lift spirits, and elevate care
To move closer to God
Honour his name
Never creating only for fame

Poetically rich means spiritually too
Financial focus no more we can do
Empty reverence harms the mind
Channel to areas that helps humankind

Loving-kindness sets us free
Poetry uplifts humanity
Our brothers, lovers, sisters, and others
Extend our hearts to open shutters

Embracing All, loving poetry speaks
To remember our each-otherness
No longer do we seek
Outside ourselves for beauty and fun
Writing poetry is where holy begun

Expressing true love from the heart
Conveys our divinity
The holy part
In ourselves is so magnificent
Writing poetry in this way celebrates it

The spirit within
Our true selves

Poetry speaks from higher realms
Engaging as one
All under the sun
Reminding us to listen,
Smell the roses, to walk,
And not run

To hear the children, and our inner voice
To observe Nature, we spontaneously rejoice
Balancing of night perfect to day
The seasons come
And we make hay

Creativity abundant to imprint life's canvas
Honouring life and love, artists use these to expand us
And the revelation of our hearts, poetry whispers, ignites a spark
Rekindles a bright and burning passion
Soul-encouraged, expresses a dimension
Our greater selves speak sagacious awareness
Magnificent elegance, grace in creation

Poetry is the perfect prayer
Portrays love and life, aware
Reflections of our true selves
Mysterious pearls bursting from shells

☆ ☆ ☆

Of all religious denominations
Non-sectarianism is key
Universal poetic breath
Is so you and me

The in-breath and out-breath
Body's intuitive tunes
Supreme intelligence
In ourselves booms

Not Hindu, not Christian, nor Sufi
Could it be
Not Buddhist, nor Jewish,
The breath, she is free
Boundless from scrutiny
To keep us alive
For each of us
Breaths to survive

Bridging worlds
The breath she does
Inner and outer
Unites as a dove
Rhythmic rider
Poetry speaks
Like the breath and the heartbeat

Connection with divinity
We strive
Poetical verse keeps hearts alive
Chiselling an open mind creation
Poetry celebrates God's sensations

People are prayers
Poems in motion
Spiritual beings
Giving Love's potion
In unique ways, sharing God's gift
Poetry contributes beautifully to this

¨♫♪ ♥ ♪♫*¨*

Our Pilot

Truth is our pilot
On the journey of life
Navigating to our destination
Amid love, amid strife

We are truth pilots
Freewill is our spark
Will we abide in Light?
Or struggle in the dark

Every day can be a good day
To please is in our hands
It is possible to lift each other up
Embrace hearts in every land

We live our lives on behalf of each other
For the truth in our hearts we stand
The feminine and the masculine lives within us
Unity and Oneness is the plan

¨♫♪ ♥ ♪♫*¨*

Grow, Grow

Every blade of grass has its angel that bends over it and whispers, 'Grow, grow.' ~ The Talmud

All life force has its energy
Supports its creation
Invisible entity

Encourages growth
Moves with time
Offers guidance
Grow, grow
Sublime

Our angel is near
A presence dear
Encoded with an essence
Our heart's steer

We're never alone
Divinity is on the throne
Directing our lives
Guiding us home

¨♫♪ ♥ ♪♫*¨*

Living with Love

Living with love, our society will know peace
By educating minds
Peace will release

Knowing people are family
Love grows
Aware of consequence
Karma flows

We move together, to the source Divine
Compassion is the religion of humankind
Diligently follow the high moral code
Greater than Gold, travelling this road

¨♫♪ ♥ ♪♫*¨*

Only the Madman

Zen Quote

Only the madman is absolutely sure
Is certain
Definite
Can't see anymore

Closed to all change
Possibilities too
No longer open
To life's issues

Attachment to knowledge
Is also not great
One of the hardest
To wipe from the slate

Freedom is knowing
Nothing is fixed
In a moment
Things change
Letting go is the trick

¨♫♪ ♥ ♪♫*¨*

Three daily Zen quotes in poem

Everyday life is the way
There is no other better way
Embrace every moment
With all your might
Establish the path
On which you take flight

Maintain the body
Keep it strong
Good health is our duty
Makes the mind clear and strong

Reality is here
To see this is clear
We are that reality
It's just you and me
We're nothing in reality
Try to understand
And, in being nothing
We are everything
All over the land

¨♫♪ ♥ ♪♫*¨*

Share Blossoms

'The most precious gift we can offer to others is our presence. When mindfulness embraces those we love, they will blossom like a flower' ~ Thich Nhat Hanh

Offer each other our presence
Engage another with our mind
Sit with all your being
Share vibrations gentle and fine

Give the gift of mindfulness
Attentive, beyond all plots
Share blossoms of loving-kindness
Human compassion hits the spot

¨♫♪ ♥ ♪♫*¨*

Be what you Love

'Let the beauty of what you love be what you do' – Rumi

Let the beauty of what you love, be what you do
Let the beauty of your expression
Come pouring steadily through

Blessed are those who have found their work
To express their beauty through
Blessed are those who know their worth
To keep on living true

Let the beauty of your heart
Take you where you need be
Let the beauty of your actions
Convey your mind with glee

What we love and what we do
Can be a hairsbreadth apart
It's up to me and it's up to you
How we use our life's spark

¨♫♪ ♥ ♪♫*¨*

Body, Mind, Spirit

'The body heals with play, the mind heals with laughter, the spirit heals with joy' ~ Anonymous.

Healing the body with play
Is the recipe today
Moving and all flowing
Within life's disarray

Heal the mind with laughter
Interpret the light of day
Find the gleam of mirth
No suppressing it come what may

The spirit heals with all the joy
In our nature's good
The spirit heals with gleeful joy
Beauty of humanity understood

¨♫♪ ♥ ♪♫*¨*

Slaves to the Vibe

Slaves to all others
We live and bow
Our lives are not ours
Transient as clouds

We live for each other
Breathe and flower
We smooth the way
Giving is power

Serving all lives
Generates vibrations
Slaves to the vibe
Life's Salvation

¨♫♪ ♥ ♪♫*¨*

In the Mirror

No point describing the moon
One must try to become it
No point pointing at the moon
We must move close and embrace it

It's easy to face the face in the mirror
Debase and disgrace it
Easily stare at our face
Distastefully deface it

Harder to find the God inside
Beaming there inside you
Harder to keep God alive
When we're arguing with every sinew

Within ourselves, our hearts rebel
Until we find the substance
Our minds are stressed
Thoughts are fenced
Until we find the essence

Of God's light
Radiating bright
In our hearts
Depression takes flight

See Dear God standing there
Reflected in the mirror

See Dear God standing there
Divine and modest
Heart shining bare

¨♫♪ ♥ ♪♫*¨*

Human Forest

How to let God live in us?
How do we let God Be?
How do we let go and let God?
How do we embody Beauty?

When God created every atom
Abides in every cell
Gauges the beats of our hearts
Is found in every shell

Such a presence is a gift we can't fathom
The living body: the temple of our soul
This sacred body is our vehicle
To do great works for humanity to excel

God is living everywhere
All around us God is there
Lighting hearts like an ember
In the Human Forest of Learning to Care

¨♫♪ ♥ ♪♫*¨*

The Story of your Soul

Never give up on speaking your truth
Ignore all others who think it's obtuse

Never give up on shining your light
Keep shining and shining, oh so bright

We are needed unique in all we do
Only one of us can make our own dreams come true

Keep following and following with all your heart
The story of your soul you need to impart

¨♫♪ ♥ ♪♫*¨*

Bright Blessings

To be honest and kind
Is the order of the day
Living truthfully
Is the only way

To create happiness
Peace
All that's good
Walk in Light
Be easily understood

Slow down our steps
Breathe the beat
See everyone
Smile and greet

In the eyes
Shines the Light
Deep within
Blessings Bright!

¨♫♪ ♥ ♪♫*¨*

Magnanimous Heart

One world community
Magnanimous heart
Embraces all people
From the start

Never misses a beat
Keeps the swing
Skips to the tune
Of living kin

All races, denominations
Live within
O magnanimous heart
You make us sing

Never turning away
From the dark
One world community
Life's true harp

¨♫♪ ♥ ♪♫*¨*

Fine Living

The magic in moments
In people who care
Magic in our daily duties
Living with dare

Delighting the downhearted
Bridging all gaps
Uplifting hearts
Love can do that

Reminds us of where we're meant to be
Loving all hearts sets us free
Harmony and dancing
Movement sublime
Create our magic
Living Fine

¨♫♪ ♥ ♪♫*¨*

Hug a stranger

Strangers are friends unmet... :-)

Let's breathe a moment
Catch our breath
Hug a stranger
Renew strength

Gain friendship
Love sublime
Golden star
Heart so kind

To hold another
Show the way
Only love
Saves the day

Uplifts our steps
Over rocky roads
Love's beauty
Fragrant rose

☆ ☆ ☆

Hug a stranger (Part II)

Hugs are an analogy for being present with others wherever you are...

Offering your loving vibrations of care, friendship, and brotherly concern even while walking along the street... without even touching or saying a word.

If your love is rejected
Again and again
When by hugging a stranger
You are considered fiend

Never give up
Keep cuddling friends
Strangers become brothers
In hugging them

Friends revealed
Can't hide away
Smiling at others
Can make one's day

Keep hugging and hugging with all your might
Friendship world created
Great humans in flight

⋆ ⋆ ⋆

Hug a stranger (Part III)

Global Family

Tenderly we hold each other
In our minds live jewels
To caress our brother

Shimmering with care
Our actions show
What lives in the heart
Makes us glow

With love and light
Life's pure delight
Bridging all gaps
Shining in the night

Holding hands
We reach the stars
Global family
This we are!

¨♫♪ ♥ ♪♫*¨*

Souls-United

Riding wonderfully warm vibrations of love
We glide, we soar, and fly like a dove
Across the mind
Peace weather
Is fine
Keep on flying
The journey of the divine

Fly onwards, forwards, upwards, free
Fly to bridge humanity
Fly with all our hearts and souls
Fly *Souls-United*
The Journey of Gold

¨♫♪ ♥ ♪♫*¨*

Soulful Dancer

'We rarely hear the inward music, but we're all dancing to it nevertheless' – Rumi

We rarely hear the inward music,
But we're dancing to it
The beat, rhythm, the tempo
Of the universe
Is within us
In all we seek

We rarely hear the inward music,
But we're dancing to it
The whirling, twirling, the movement
Of our splendid souls
Creative compassion
Through the hand that gives

We rarely hear the inward music,
But we're dancing to it
Our hearts are guides
Intuition flies
To the beat
Honouring all that is

¨♫♪ ♥ ♪♫*¨*

Humans

To my family everywhere
do you feel my smile?
Beaming directly into your heart
Let me stay a while

Though we may live far away
Our breath is very close
Breathing in or breathing out
We are connected in this style

On the in-breath
Or on the out
Our lives are linked by life
From moment to moment
We breathe as one
Humans sharing this life

¨♫♪♥♪♫*¨*

Fits like a Glove

Inspired poetry
A blessing
Free
Magically oozing
Through you and me

The subject
Poem
The meaning
Theme
Dashes through the mind
And fingers unseen

Manifesting itself
Through rhythm and verse
Revealing life's potions
To sufferings' curse

Enter into the kingdom
Of God's Love
Divinity within
And, surrounding
Fits like a glove

¨♫♪ ♥ ♪♫*¨*

Forgiveness: The Kingdom of Clear Sight

Beyond right and wrong
There is a song
Of friendship held at bay
Anchored at a shore
Forevermore
Until forgiveness shows the way

Turbulent winds strong opinions brings
Our inner compass turns upright
Emotions take flight
The mind in blight
Seems impossible to see right:
Blue birds of happiness have all taken fright

Beyond right and wrong
Freedom is clear
We do no harm to others
Experiences steer
Karmic retributions
Cosmic forces take pact
We mean so more to each other
Beyond this and that

Anchored at the shore
Forevermore
The gift of absolution
For us to explore
The moment we do it
We set ourselves right
Forgiveness is the Kingdom of Clear Sight

¨♫♪ ♥ ♪♫*¨*

Blessing All Hearts

A Buddha sits with mind affixed
On the breath, in and out
As one

Observes vibrations
Rising, falling sensations
Without attaching to any one

Understands the nature
Of the pain and pleasant caper
Impermanence the underlying tune

For every living being
Compassion is needed brimming
In our hearts right now, not soon

¨♫♪ ♥ ♪♫*¨*

Life's Plate

Never quite as we expect to be
Life of ours
And, us
So free

We shape the plate
Dexterously
Create some tastes
To help us see

All the nutrients keep us alive
Equip us with the will to survive
The body an amazing vehicle
Our minds are truly a miracle

Creates patterns in our lives
Our minds, our guides to breathe this jive
To nurture, surrender, and survive
Keeping beating hearts alive

¨♫♪ ♥ ♪♫*¨*

Awaiting a friend

Awaiting a friend
Who's really a friend
Never a foe will do
A friend that's true
Really true
Never let a bad deed befall you

Awaiting a friend
Who's really a friend
Any old soul will do

One who's seen the light
Of true human might
The spirit that's in you

Such a friend
Ushers to mend
The pain deep within

Pain that's silent
Deep grief quiet
Loves deep inside
To heal you

¨♫♪ ♥ ♪♫*¨*

Thoughts Personified

We are the example to ourselves
Our mistakes talk, our soul rebels
Tugging and taking us where we should go
To learn our lessons
Sprout and grow

We are the teachers of our own hearts
Students to all others, the gifts they impart
Guiding and taking us brilliantly in
The beauty of our splendid kin

Being the taskmaster of our lives
Inspires deeply the will to survive
Never any blame to cause someone
We are the reason for what is done

Thoughts personified in all we do
Actions make our living see-through
Clear as crystal, there we are
The ripple effect spreads near and far

¨♫♪ ♥ ♪♫*¨*

Everywhere

Everywhere around us
Life constantly displays love
Incites action in our living
Effortlessly issues love worth giving

Compels us to reach deep inside
Overlook any need to hide
Dismiss all debris full of pride
Bare feathers of a bird that glides

Freely in the air of the mind
Entertain impressions of the sublime
Create a full and wonderful experience
Expressing life, in all its magnificence

¨♫♪ ♥ ♪♫*¨*

The Cat and The Rat

If the rat and the cat can do it
Then why oh why can't we?
If two assumed enemies can come together
Then what is it with humanity?

When a simple cat can reduce his ego
To live without separating fear
When a courageous rat can overcome timidity
To in fact, take over and steer

Then why oh why do some humans create so much mess and strife?
Why oh why do some humans dismiss the meaning of life?

Soft and sensitive is our true nature
Gentleness is our gift
Thank you to the cat and the rat
For reminding us of this

¨♫♪ ♥ ♪♫*¨*

If Only ...

No matter how hard we try
We'll never meet some people in the eye
With all of life's twists and turns
Peace with others we often yearn

Chemical reactions in our minds
Attraction or repulsion is their charm
Observe these sensations in ourselves
Are we truly under a spell?

To act beyond our kinder ways
To forget that love can save the day
To think before we say those words
No one need ever yell

Or curl the tone of loving-kindness
When sometimes ignorance does blind us
To be the saviour of our minds
To take meter every time

If only we could really try
To see the apple in every eye
To embrace dear heaven in our hearts
Dance and celebrate the love in us

¨♫♪ ♥ ♪♫*¨*

Not me, not me, only you, only you

Not me, not me, only you, only you
With this determination
All hearts will come through

Spiritually driven
To set us free
Underlying inspiration
To let each other be

The best of ourselves
Talented layered pearls
Elevate spirits
With the stories we tell

Portraying hearts
Expressing life's spark
There is no reason to live in the dark
Set our sights on surrounding flames
All of us beacons in every domain

Guides to each other
To let love live
Embracing the Light
We're living with

¨♫♪ ♥ ♪♫*¨*

A Little Bit More

'Four short words sum up what has lifted most successful individuals above the crowd: a little bit more. They did all that was expected of them and a little bit more.' - A. Lou Vickery

A little bit
And a little bit more
Another bit
And then some more

To do the job
And get it done
To successful individuals
These words do sum

Up the motivation
To do it right
Fruitfully
Giving all your might

To do a bit
A little bit more
Reaching the end
Without a flaw

¨♫♪ ♥ ♪♫*¨*

Freedom

Freedom is good
Freedom is divine
Freedom is the state
Of living in time

With all nature
Abiding in cue
Ever listening
To intuitive tunes

Bio-rhythms, tempo
Our inner heart's beat
The body, our temple
Never sleeps

Our minds have the freedom
To spend the time
Creating and celebrating in
This Mystery sublime

¨♫♪ ♥ ♪♫*¨*

A Mind of its Own

Every being in the world
Has a mind of its own
Driven to follow its purpose
Filled with instinct
Or conscious choices

Determined to move in a true way
A rhythm indicating which way
Spontaneous movements or decisions
The blessing of life we are given

Freewill is a human banner
Intellectual understanding
We sometimes flounder
Emotions are beyond us
When every hour is so rushed

Take time to watch animals
Awake in the moment
Expandable
Our greatest teachers live simply
Amongst us, completely

¨♫♪ ♥ ♪♫*¨*

The Courage of Humans

Calling all poets
Around the globe
Lift your voices
Garnish the flow
Of the Mind
Share its depths
Reach out to others
Time well spent

Take into your heart
Our human part
That hides under covers
Won't make a start
Inspire a passion
To turn the key
Open the door
And, you are free

To speak our minds
To take our steps
Forwards and onwards
A skip often leapt
Into the unknown
Fearlessly bound
In the courage of humans
A jewel is found

¨♫♪ ♥ ♪♫*¨*

Already Won

How will this ever end?
Persecution is a human trend
In the mind of oneself
Shaking the core of mental wealth

When health is wealth
Being mentally strong
Mindfully able to get along
With each moment
Whatever it brings
Even in heartache, we know how to sing

And share ourselves
Mind's true worth
With each other
Especially oneself

Peace and kindness
Issuing loving fineness
Courageously giving love that binds us

In the heart, in our deeds
The mind: it guides
Is our best steed
To ride upon
Life's true song
The journey, the destination
Gifts already won

¨♫♪ ♥ ♪♫*¨*

Really nice moments

Really nice moments
Are only seconds away
Seconds away
To make your day
Fashion your mind in your unique way
Shaping it as you play

Really nice moments
Are already here
Already here
To bring you cheer
Gifting you with ability bright
Steering oneself with love's insight

Really nice moments
Can be here to stay
Mixed amongst life's fluctuating maze
Consciously choose them in how we think
Really nice moments: a living gift

¨♫♪ ♥ ♪♫*¨*

Feelings

The fullness of feelings
Away from misgivings
Makes moments complete

I feel alive
I will to survive
Life is a treat

Feeling feelings
Life is living
Harmony in the heart

My home is beaming
Because I am gleaming
The essence of life's spark

¨♫♪ ♥ ♪♫*¨*

When we look closer

Beware of the dogs at the gate
Faces ferocious
Eyes of slate
Don't even try to test your fate
Best to stay clear
Of the dogs at the gate

Rearrange your life
Abate the gate
Do everything in your power
Don't give those dogs bait

Stay away, hesitate
Those dogs know how to keep you at bay
But then again
Who are they?
Are they truly, what they convey

Take a step closer, peek inside
Are those dogs even alive?
Stone structures etched with skilful hands
These dogs they come from moulded sand!

Oh my, oh my, these dogs are good
Cleverly made, it's now understood
Things are not always as they seem
When we look closer, the truth can be seen

¨♫♪ ♥ ♪♫*¨*

The Bird is Free

Life is oh so serious
Sharing poems may alleviate us
From all the tensions and the strife
To discover meaning, and feel blithe

Going beyond sounds sounding wrong
Discovering tunes to a different song
Gentler vibrations, message, and tones
Engaging the senses, bringing them home

In our hearts
The bird is free
To sing and speak of liberty
Holding hands within our minds
Peace, love, and freedom
Shines!

¨♫♪ ♥ ♪♫*¨*

My Heart

What in my heart, do I want to do?
To express my heart
To feel it true
To be love
To sing with grace
Ever showing my real face

How in my heart will I muster to be?
A life illuminating sanity
Courageously giving wholesome love
Fluttering butterfly, peaceful dove

¨♫♪ ♥ ♪♫*¨*

Roses

Outside my window is the tallest rose
Stands proudly
Elegant pose
Pink rose
Its petals
Pink
Soft and gentle
A sight to seek

Ushering goodness
Tenderness fair
Blesses all eyes that see her there

Standing tall
Beauty galore
Opens the senses
To take in more

Of her light
Blessing bright
One knows it when breathing right
With your heart
Take her in
Smell the beauty of her kin

Queen of flowers
The rose she stands
Beauty of this given land

A gift, love's promise
In your hand
Reaches the heart of any man

¨♫♪ ♥ ♪♫*¨*

Feel It Thinking

Challenge our thinking
Question it too
Observe the habits we slip into

Repeating actions
Because we can
Over and over
Ingrained in the hand

Of all we do
And what we say
How we deliver it
In what way

Keeping harmony of the mind
Is surely the goal of humankind
To shake, imbalance, and keep it away
Dismisses the peace present today

Among ourselves and deep within
We help each other learn to sing
With our kin, follow the light
Into matters of deep insight
Knowledge and compassion strongly link
Increase to feel in everything we think

¨♫♪ ♥ ♪♫*¨*

Writing of Trees

Writing of trees
In the summer
Breeze
Their leaves
Etching
The air

Their barks
Are our paper
To write
Our heart's caper
A blessing
So very fair

The roots of their giving
Reach down deeply living
Foundations of this earth

Grounding our writing
Essence enlightening
Embracing hearts
Spreading mirth

¨♫♪ ♥ ♪♫*¨*

Allowing the Love

Emotions aren't real when they steal so much of your time
And, mind
Making you blind
To those unkind

Untrue
In all they do
Actions go against you
All you stand for
Love and adore

Like freedom
Truth
Light-hearted flute
Body a temple only for good
Voice of gold
As we grow old
Ushering beauty never sold

Invaluable riches flow freely
Living like this is so easy
Allowing, allowing, allowing the love
Our only duty
To make life less tough

¨♫♪ ♥ ♪♫*¨*

Each Moment is Our Star

All good things must come to an end
Just why is that like so?

And this too, this too shall pass
No point in making an issue

No constant but change
All change no constant
Impermanence is the truth

Everything arises to pass away
Fluxing fluctuations
Vibrations pace

Always changing
Never the same
Unrepeatable
This moment is

Potentially magical
Each moment can create more
Living in a space

Without attachment
Aware of the hatching
Of binding, that harms the heart
Imbued with Loving-Kindness
Wakefully guiding us
Each Moment is Our Star

¨♫♪ ♥ ♪♫*¨*

As the breeze blows

Inspiration flows as the breeze blows
One moment it's here
The next it goes
Best to be right
On your toes
Awake
Ever-present
When the breeze blows

¨♫♪ ♥ ♪♫*¨*

True Meaning

Living in a world where most language is silent
Non-verbal communication
True meaning resides in
Through actions, movements
Expressions and behaviour
Our bodies display our inner mind's flavour

All words we deliver, our actions instil
Are we only performing for a good karmic bill?
Or do feelings go deeper to the bone
Driven by a greater destined tone

The questions, the answers
The conversations and prose
None of them needed
With our actions on show

¨♫♪ ♥ ♪♫*¨*

Gratitude to poems

I can't stop writing poems
My muse is always going
Subtle treasures move right through me
The page is where they're set free

May they come and find you
Into your hearts may they bind true
Adding some more love and affection
Inspire to give our brothers more attention

And, engagement of our presence
Every moment full of significance
When the transfer of vibrations
Uplifts in their deliverance

I can't stop writing poems
My muse is always going
Is this how it is when a seed blossoms from sowing?

¨♫♪ ♥ ♪♫*¨*

Loving All

Loving All
Loving more
Loving ever after
Despite it all

Loving all
Not only some
Loving people
Everyone

Loving rats
Loving cats
Contented
Sitting on our laps to pat

Loving flights
Loving rights
Taken on rebellious plights

To speak the truth
Of all our love
Bravery stands
In loving love

¨♫♪ ♥ ♪♫*¨*

Actions for Love

Actions for reward
Almost deletes action at all
When not coming from the right place
Actions can be cold

Actions for love
Imparts love from the heart
Bursting with substance
Actions spark

Goodwill for others
Care for fellow man
Time to show we really give a damn
To take them or leave them
No longer can we do
Actions are needed for our dreams to come true

In the labour of love, actions are great
Fruits from which to celebrate
We may not see them
But they are there
Blossoming in the eyes of those who care

¨♫♪ ♥ ♪♫*¨*

Smile Deep Inside

It's hard to fill an empty heart
Empty in a lonely dark
That insists its presence, in the light of day
Struggles with love's brighter way

Happy with unhappy
Vibrations and such
Agitations rise from a slight brush
With the truth
Speak if you dare
Ruffle feathers because you care

About what's right, just, and fair
A moral code, an ethical flair
Sing and dance, live its tune
Living in a way unhappy hearts may soon
Smile from down deep inside
Open up broad and live life wide

¨♫♪ ♥ ♪♫*¨*

Beauty Deep Inside

Invisible to some
But not to others
Appearances change
As one discovers

What we see
Comes from ourselves
The way we view
Our interpretations tell

Beauty comes from deep inside
The beholder's eye is where beauty shines
It's how we see that truly matters
Rise above life that flatters

Look around
Absorb each other
Take the time to *see* another
Reach in deep
Find the light
Beauty shining clear and bright

¨♫♪ ♥ ♪♫*¨*

Sing Through

Moving on
Finding a new song
Exploring avenues
Developing fresh fronds

On the path of life
Its twisty turns
Smoothing round the bends
Soothing hurt

Embrace the new times
People too
Release the old
Remove the glue

With less attachment
To all we do
Our life, free-flowing
We can sing through

¨♫♪ ♥ ♪♫*¨*

Set Love Free

We're all humans
This we are
Colours flourishing
Near and far

Similarities not distant
We all have scars
Living life
No holds barred

Sometimes we won't get along
With another's way of song
Chords so different they make a gong
When delicates sounds, you wish upon

We're all humans
This we are
Embracing brothers
Chasing stars

With all our differences
Seek harmony
Find heart's happiness
Set love free

¨♫♪ ♥ ♪♫*¨*

Infinite Self

'Liberation through Self-realisation is the first and foremost aim, yet at the same time the welfare of the universe is what follows next not as a duty, but as a consequence of love which emanates spontaneously out of the realisation of oneness with the universe. Hence it is not just helping or serving others, but rather loving others, knowing them to be our own Self' ~ The Living God – A Biography of Bhagavan

Through realising our Self
We fall in love with All
Such enlightening understanding liberates us
Enabling our love to excel

The care of the universe
Becomes our greatest task
Our oneness with others inspires us
To make the universe unsurpassed

Salvation of the universe
Is the saving of ourselves
Liberation comes through our true Self
Permeating loving-kindness that will last

¨♫♪ ♥ ♪♫*¨*

A Maze

As a continuous flow
Samsara goes
Repeating the cycle of life

Past, present and future
Each lifetime suits us
Determined by actions we sow

Birth, life and death
Our souls seem to digress
Into perpetual wandering

Journeying through lifetimes
A quest of humankind
To come out of all suffering

Embracing unity
Our oneness with all things
Is a potential, real way

To shatter the illusion
Separation does bring
When we're united, we're freed from Samsara's maze

¨♫♪ ♥ ♪♫*¨*

Bright Blessings
Haiku

A String of Words

A string of words
A strand of pearls
Prominent around your neck

Our walk
In a vase
Hibiscus flower

Deep-sleep cycle
I awake
Refreshed

Sunset
Sunrise
Illuminated bookends to deep, deep night

Hands of a friend
Hands of an angel
Same, same

I can do it all
I imagine
From my seat

Lifting off the ground
A flock of sparrows
Fan the sky

Circling great sky
Pelicans in a V
Glide silently

So much to say
Rain drops
On pond

Writing on water
Rain drops
Etch and bubble

¨♫♪ ♥ ♪♫*¨*

Life Goes On

In the distance
Barking dogs, a train
And, me

Moving across the lawn
My cat and his shadow
I love them both

High in the mountains
Rolling plains
And, cows

Driving on a country road
Exquisite scenery
Speeds by my window

Sun-shadows dance
Along busy streets
Life goes on

Taking time
To take in the views
When to stop?

Embracing change
I slowly undress
Autumn tree

Carpeting the ground
Cherry blossoms
Last night's rain

In the blue sky
Altering jigsaws
Clouds at play

'All is well'
Birds chirp
From dawn to dusk

¨♫♪ ♥ ♪♫*¨*

Beacon

Hot springs
Running river
Heavy rain on the street

After the rain
Dancing pond
Mirroring sky

Gazing in puddle
Perfect sky
Reflects

Swiftly
Horse-shaped clouds
Gallop across the sky

My dog, my horse, my rat
Cloud-shaped memories
Float by high

Warming my face
Penetrating my heart
The Sun

Clothed by warmth
Naked
Summer robes

Dancing in the breeze clothes on the line

Lighthouse beacons
Sun lights
Friendship ignites our lives

Waving goodnight
Palm trees
In the breeze

¨♫♪ ♥ ♪♫*¨*

Labyrinth

Rain drops
In puddles
Many mandalas

Labyrinth beauty
Spider web
On my window

What more can I say?
Clear blue
Endless sky

Expressionless
Gray sky
Difficult to read

Knocking on sky
'Come in,' sky answers
Room for everyone

Amidst clouds
Circle of blue
Dive through

Cloud origami
Decorates
Sky ceiling

Perfectly placed
Everything in nature
Leaves on a tree

'Fall!'
Shouted the thunder
To the rain

At the liquor store
Rows upon rows
Of sore heads

¨♫♪ ♥ ♪♫*¨*

Wings

Blowing in the wind
Leaves, flowers
And, our thoughts

Fluctuating moments
Capture on film
A shadow

On the earth
Elephants tread
Softly

Written words
Travel world
When legs cannot

Roadside puddles
Shallow pools mirror
Great sky heights

Clouds billow blue sky
Shapes moving effortlessly
Across our mindscape

Prayer flags
Wishes
In the wind

Purple haze
In rows
Lavender

Among weeds
Dandelion
Smiling

Lying on the ground
My jumper's
Shadow

In the sky
Magic
And, clouds

¨♫♪ ♥ ♪♫*¨*

Phases

Branches reach up
Tree life
Hands in the air

Shapes and shadows
Leaf impressions
At dusk

Pink pastels
On blue
As night approaches

Quiet
The space between
Twilight

Lone bird
Sings
Voice in the dark

Distant sounds
Life
Ongoing

Night light
Penetrates darkness
Revelation

Moon saucer
Beams its presence
From every angle

At night
Earth cools
Restful breathing

Flickering sunlight
Iridescent horizon
Sunrise

Expired sunlight
On the ground
Autumn leaves

¨♫♪ ♥ ♪♫*¨*

Dancing

Leaf shadows on the ground
Dance in sunlight
Blown by wind

Bird shrieks
So much activity
Above our heads

Always conducting
Tree branches
Negotiating the wind

Tree leaves rustle
In waves
Loudly, softly

All of a sudden
Wind chaos
Then quiet

So much movement!
No wonder
Tree roots anchor deep

Melody outside my window
Tree music
Harmony by birds

Riding on a branch
Where are we going?
Bird asks tree

Nature's make-up
Sunlight shimmers
On smooth green leaf faces

So friendly
Leaves waving
In the wind

Dressed for the dance
Palm trees
In hula-skirts

¨♫♪ ♥ ♪♫*¨*

Healing Hope Bird

One-legged teal Drake
Finds refuge
In our front yard

Hot sun drains
Duck pond
From roadside

Heavy rain returns
Roadside duck pond
Bubbling springs

Assortment of birds
Ply for seed
By the water bowl

Nectar bird
Swoops to overwhelm
Big black raven

Bird colours flurry
Front lawn
Feeding

Bird calls
Highlight the moment
Wonder

Safe
Little rat
Curled in my lap

Summer winds
Blow away
Winter chills

Climbing Healing Hill
Hope
Carries me last stretch

¨♫♪ ♥ ♪♫*¨*

Fresh Thoughts

Break from tradition
Weather patterns are changing
Everything's doing it!

Leaves wave
Fresh thoughts
Blowing in the breeze

Bird song on wind
Town criers everywhere
In the not too heavy rain

White skies
Intermission
At the movies

Bird calls
Vocalise
The moment

Sweeping dirt
The pigeons
Sort for seeds

Emotions
Windy day
Cloudy, sunny, rain

Love,
Slippery
Tender fruit

Lightening cracks
Hearts open
Finally

A place in life
Bridge
Between two hearts

Musical Tree
Full of birds
Happiness

¨♫♪ ♥ ♪♫*¨*

Floating Blossoms

Canopy for our mind
The sky, the heavens
The galaxies and beyond

Let's paint the sky blue
Cloud swirls here
And, a splash of sun

Rainy night
Street lights
Ignite pathway in puddle

Raindrops on branches
Glistening crystals
Transient beauty

'Fall faster'
Heavy rain says
To autumn leaves

Spider web threads
Guitar strings in the breeze
Silently strum

Woven in air
Silken mandala
Catching spider dreams

In a bubble
Breathing air
Life is very precious

Time flies floating blossoms

Alive
The child within
No matter our age

¨♫♪ ♥ ♪♫*¨*

www.ingramcontent.com/pod-product-compliance
Ingram Content Group UK Ltd.
Pitfield, Milton Keynes, MK11 3LW, UK
UKHW041313190726
13845UKWH00025B/236

9 788182 534957